Money Should Be Fun

"Isn't it amazing—everybody has everybody's number
and yet everything keeps going along."

WILLIAM HAMILTON

Money Should Be Fun

with an Introduction by

JOHN KENNETH GALBRAITH

HOUGHTON MIFFLIN COMPANY   BOSTON   1980

To Mrs. Average

Library of Congress Cataloging in Publication Data

Hamilton, William, date
    Money should be fun.

    1. Money—Caricatures and cartoons.   2. American wit and humor, Pictorial.   I. Title.
NC1429.H324A4 1980   741.5'973   79-26812
ISBN 0-395-28218-7
ISBN 0-395-29319-7 pbk.

Printed in the United States of America

P 10 9 8 7 6 5 4 3 2 1

Of the 189 drawings in this collection, 28 originally appeared in *The New Yorker,* and were copyrighted © 1976, 1977, 1978, and 1979 by The New Yorker Magazine, Inc.

Eight of the drawings were syndicated by Chronicle Features, © 1976 and 1977 by Chronicle Publishing Co.

"Listen—I have to run around and connect some things because this day's gone berserk."

Introduction

by John Kenneth Galbraith

My attention, I'm convinced, was captured by the very first Hamilton drawing I ever saw. It was of business executives at work or, more precisely, continuing their work in ostentatious relaxation over the sauce. For me the study of the American executive at work, at play and at thought has been for a lifetime the most compelling branch of anthropology, more interesting on balance than the Fiji Islanders, United States Senators or even my fellow economists. I knew, instantly, that I had in Hamilton a colleague who saw what I saw but with the ability to define it that, sadly and totally, I lacked. The well-tailored, underexercised, vaguely overfed bodies were there, as also the loosening skin around the necks and chins. And the superb contentment, assurance and satisfaction with self. And best of all, the artist's exact ear for what they were saying. Vanity is often involved in one's response to art as to humor. Hamilton had nudged mine; he was affirming that what I had seen, or thought I had seen, was completely right.

William Hamilton's executives are, I believe, his highest art. But some think he is even better on overachieving and dangerously educated youth. I'm not going to quarrel. His young wives are beautifully rendered—slim, modish, emotionally intense, elaborately dim. And equally well-considered are their men. Their hair is right; soon they will be overweight; one or two have always a fraudulent aspect of deep insight; all on closer examination are content in their failure to follow the speaker in her current flight from reality.

One or two of the young men are always exquisite in their well-groomed, uncomprehending stupidity. I do not, for obvious reasons of age and association, know these people as well as the executives. But I do know that they exist. So if someone insists that Hamilton is really the Grant Wood of the American overachiever, I will not object.

Once William Hamilton did a drawing of some businessmen in relaxed satisfaction over the fact that I had never met a payroll. Vanity again. I thanked him, instead of, like Kissinger or Churchill, demanding that this deprecating work be destroyed. But I had never met the artist until, one day, I got a letter from him asking if I would write this introduction. I spent a whole morning wondering how such a superb draftsman could have such awful handwriting. Then I hastened to accept. Once some years ago I wrote a note of introduction for a book of drawings by David Levine. He and Herbert Block (Herblock), with William Hamilton, understand best the social purpose of this art form. It is of little natural value for comforting the afflicted. But it is truly great for afflicting the comfortable. It's a privilege to have had association with two of the three masters. Vanity again, but show me the man who, similarly favored, would suppress it.

"Tom, the boy is over John Kenneth Galbraith and ready to go to work."

"And Always Hang Out with High-Energy People"

"O.K. now, Jessica, the number before the dot is a five and the one after a ten. What time is it?"

"Promise you'll never, ever tell. My real name's not Mary. My real name's Cloud Flower."

"I mean, I LIKE America, but my first allegiance will always be to outer space."

"I know just how you feel. We have two punks and a Moonie."

"I'm sorry, Daddy, but Yale just isn't strong enough in weaving."

"I don't know what I'm going to do. I'm not underprivileged enough for a scholarship."

"Gosh, Mrs. Phillips—you look so young for somebody so old!"

"Did it ever occur to you, Mother, I may not want to live with anybody yet?"

"Your son just opened a boutique!"

"Well, young lady—this is the last time I bother serving you something real!"

"You were such an adorable baby."

"Marriage? Are You Crazy — I Love You!"

"That's not true. I've never waffled about loving you."

"I love this part where it's all still nice."

"Don't worry, darling. You'll happen."

"Darling, let's not talk about solar heating tonight."

"I'm sorry, Matthew; you have style—but Niven has substance."

"My God, I think your then husband is my now husband."

"I'm so glad I met you while I'm still just blocking
out my life."

"Do you really love me or is it just this WATS line?"

"Hi, Barbara, remember me? Guess what—I'm incorporated and I bought a co-op!"

"Thank you, Ted. I think you've evolved a lot, too."

"Wow—you mean you have your very own, Private Moral Universe?"

"Look, I don't mind being just a panacea—as long as there aren't any other panaceas."

"The woman I live with doesn't understand me."

"Is that too much to ask for, Angela? A little leverage?"

"I asked her to marry me. She said she'd get back to me."

"Have you noticed how well our selves are getting along?"

"So this is adultery!"

"Can't we just be friends and lovers and leave it at that?"

"At Least He's Appreciating."

"So far we're just revelling in each other's minds."

"He's a lawyer—but for nice things."

"He's very much like Leo Tolstoy, except he doesn't write."

"He made a dulcimer and played it for me one summer evening—the air smelling of lawn, sparkling with fireflies. And I said to myself, 'Why am I listening to this awful music?'"

"I'm staying completely out of it, which has made getting
information sheer hell."

"I don't know—a brain surgeon just sounds smarter than
an orthopedic surgeon."

"Did I ever just get out in time! Now I hear he's trying to get his hair back holistically."

"He's a smoldering banker."

"At first he was a hopeless romantic. Then, just hopeless."

"I got what I wanted, but it wasn't what I expected."

"Something Is Wrong. There's Not Enough Pressure Today."

"I've just graduated from the Stanford Business School
and I'm a workaholic."

"For ten grand they don't get a concept; they just get an idea."

"I told Mrs. Hayne how desperately this board wanted a woman."

"How little we really own, Tom, when you consider all there is to own."

"I'm sorry—he's shoveling funds into offshore accounts at the moment."

"Now. What are we looking for? We are looking for the intelligent, well-educated, high-income dog owner."

"Fernando, you know the conglomerate worships you as a designer. We're just not sure you're ready for a scent."

"I mean, you can have the cleanest air in the world, but if you can't manufacture anything what the hell good is it?"

"I'm not the kind of man to blow my own horn. That's why I'm hiring you to blow it."

"He did pick up the ball and run with it. He ran to another shop with it."

"Great news! I've located a complete idiot."

"I'm afraid you have the wrong locker room. This is administration."

"I just wanted to say, sir, that I couldn't agree more with what you said in there about me being a sycophant."

"Now, remember—we're only after the top 50 per cent of humanity!"

"I think things are beginning to get serious. He's invited us to meet his parent company."

"I've learned a lot in sixty-three years. But, unfortunately, almost all of it is about aluminum."

"That's it! 'A new kind of newness!'"

"You know, I'm actually from down there someplace."

"Safety? Of course we're committed to safety—we're committed to safety and any other damn thing that sells cars."

"Would a study shut them up?"

"Unfortunately, the Marriage Was Nothing Like the Wedding."

"I am not pushing your buttons. As a matter of fact you are pushing my buttons!"

"Having a baby really puts a cat in perspective."

"What do I think? I think I wish *Roots* had never been written."

"Look. Let's at least stay together until the Crockers'
party."

"I'd like to share about why you called me a
turkey."

"You're a complete waste of fresh rosemary!"

"I do, again."

"Francis, shouldn't we buy something digital?"

"You're using me, Harold—you're using me and you're using the whales."

"No, Henry—inflation is the No. 2 problem. YOU are the No. 1 problem."

"I'm sick of it, Martha. Sick of the intense scrutiny, the acute criticism, the occasional flurries of *haute cuisine*, and the unending little sardonic smile."

"But think of the people who like us as a couple."

"The bank is satisfied with me, Princeton is satisfied with me, I'm satisfied with me—what on earth is holding you back?"

"I know it's Monday morning quarterbacking, Muff, but I'd like a divorce."

"And another thing—I do not act this way just because
I'm a banker. Eugene O'Neill was no sweetheart either."

"I've been thinking about your anger. Maybe you should
go back to bottling it up."

"Well, against the odds, here we are—Fran, her ex, me, my ex, Dick, my ex's new, Phil, Fran's ex's new, Pearl, Fran's ex's ex, David, Fran's ex's ex's new. CHEERS!"

"We Think Money Should Be Fun."

"First it's sex, then money; then you weed out, simplify, and you find power is enough."

"Having a fine old name really has been enough for me."

"It's not just money, boys—it's also people. Money's worthless unless it allows you to manipulate people."

"Money is life's report card."

"Mr. Hayne, Sam, has been a member since before the club went to hell."

"Poor Henry just discovered Bjorn Borg makes more money than he does."

"Of course, there were years of anonymity before we were recognized as young collectors."

"Sure it would be great to be rich and famous—but I don't know, rich may be enough."

"But I think Charles's greatest legacy was simply money."

"I paid my dues—and nothing happened!"

"When I said, 'Where are we and where are we going?' I did not mean financially!"

"The dollar and I seem to be weakening at the same rate."

"'What's money?' he used to say. Unfortunately, he never did find out."

"Oh, if I hadn't got into stocks, I suppose I might have got into something completely different. Bonds, maybe, warrants, options, futures . . . who knows?"

"We're trying to choose a car that doesn't make a statement."

"Some of us are just born with the knack of inheriting."

"Money is just a way to make other people look dumb."

"Commercial Art for Commercial Art's Sake!"

"I tell you, the book has everything—sex, history, consciousness, and cats!"

"He's bankrupt—he was 100 per cent committed
in Op art."

"Oh, I've got talent, all right, but I've never found anyone who could really exploit me."

"Sean—come say hello—here's exactly you, except published!"

"I haven't actually been published or produced yet. But I have had some things professionally typed."

"It's going to be a kind of Woody Allen autobiographical film, and I'm looking for a Diane Keaton figure."

"Without business, who the hell could afford art?"

"I'll let him get back to you as soon as he's cranked something out."

"Without adultery and alcoholism, there would be no art."

"Did you think a lot as a child?"

"I love it, Sean. It's more than 'House and Garden,' but it's not TOO 'History of Art.'"

"Many write books, Connell, but only a few write properties."

"At last, I'm a hack!"

"You Knew I Didn't Want to See My Life Etched Against a Backdrop of Modern Suburbia."

"Sorry it's such a mess. Our pool man died over the weekend."

"I hear you call me the 'wiry little jock.'"

"Cream is not a bright dog,
but Cream is a sweet dog—
aren't you, Cream!"

"We love the country. But I still feel threatened by the garden."

"We met at a Cuisinart seminar."

"The veggies are from Sue's garden and the vino is from my winery."

"Eliza? Oh, please say you two haven't eaten. I've just had the most horrendous Cuisinart overrun."

"Now, on this wall, I see books—not heavy books, but light books: beige books, salmon books, biscuit and pink books..."

"Maybe it senses your anger."

"This will be fun—we've found you can tell everything
about new people by the way they play."

"We couldn't stand the heat, so we got out of the kitchen."

"I thought while it's still light you might like to pop out and see my compost."

"My God, You Can Shop!"

"I'm not looking for a personality. I'm looking for a blue suit."

"Have you got something a little more . . . hard-nosed?"

"Now. Have you already got the coffee table?"

"Do you sell anything that doesn't have 'middle-class' written all over it?"

"Oh, I understand. 'Resource' means a place like Saks or something."

"Mr. Gorman, you look like a million dollars, such as it looks today."

"It's his fortieth birthday. I'm looking for something natural."

"Now, did you want to see the real or the authentic?"

"I wonder if shopping will ever be recognized as a medium."

"Sue, Do You Remember
My Hair?"

"It's too weird! Same school, same college, same bank.
What was your ex-wife's name?"

"Sometimes I wonder—what if you actually had become
a folk singer and I had had my ears pierced?"

"I know I'm authentic. But lately I feel like a reproduction."

"Well, that's over. Now we're a cute couple people met in Bermuda."

"I've always had a warm spot for Denver. I was consecrated in Denver."

"Aerospace, pharmaceuticals, marriage—I got into
every one of them just when the game was over."

"Nobody realized I was a man to watch until it was too late."

"Look, just because I was your favorite teacher doesn't mean you were my favorite student."

"Which is it this time—your fumble in the Princeton game or your first marriage?"

"So many of my rejects seem to improve with time."

"Actually, I'm just coming down off a kind of surprising haircut, and I think I'll just hang around the house for a while."

"I don't know where we went wrong. Everything we bought was in the Museum of Modern Art."

"I just don't know how much more I can take sitting around out here with nothing to hype."

"People used to say to me, 'Do you play basketball?'
Now they say, 'Did you play basketball?'"

"Why do you suppose so few of us have managed to hang onto our youth this way?"

"It's not just you, dear—the other astronauts are getting older, too."

"Just a Simplistic Salad, Hans."

"We're Midwestern nobodies—seat us with the lepers."

"If she's not the one and he's not the one, who are they?"

"It'll be all right, man. My car has stabilizer bars."

"I think I'd rather be here than anywhere—except maybe in Beverly Hills with Warren Beatty."

"And there you are too, some nice chicken soup."

"They're your bodies of course, but have you counted these carbo's?"

"I know that's not his daughter, because I'm his daughter."

"Now by 'society' do you mean mankind or just us?"

"I Collect People. They're in Here."

"I know exactly what you mean. Sometimes I just turn the radio on FM and think, think, think."

"We think it was very hip of you to ask us together."

"Old-Fashioneds used to be Fred's Achilles' heel. Now Margaritas are Fred's Achilles' heel."

"Here comes the black hole in my universe."

"Excuse me—I've been trying lately to listen to what my body is telling me and it just suggested I pop over and introduce myself."

"I'm into the takeover aspect of corporate law— but I still play the guitar."

"Get him on opera or baseball and he's fine."

"I keep forgetting we're the same age."